FIEND CURLS

Epiphanies Weaved Into Prose and Poetry

ISHRAT PARVEEN

For the Wolf and Phoenix

Biting her lips so hard they started to bleed
Another blow, another whip
The fury she'd never seen

This was never the love she wanted or need
Another sigh she heaved

As he turned his back on her and decided to leave
She found love in the ways she couldn't believe
But couldn't decipher why they ended blue purple and green
Losing herself into his darkness
She was guarding the only precious thing he gave her in
the moment of heat

Daddy loves you,
Whispered to the baby
Like a lullaby it'd make him fall asleep

The scars on her skin told a story
One she never wanted to recite
Hiding them with the layers of pretense
Which too was powerless as her will

Mistress of her prowess
Unaware that he saw right through her facade
Playing his cards like an Ace
She still stood tall to protect her pup
Fighting the rejection of her mate

The tremors of fear hearing his footsteps
Gave her a nauseating feeling
As she ran to throw up everything
Heaving a sigh followed by a hiccup

Of the foreseeing sob that left her mouth
Sinking in her sorrows, getting engulfed
In the darkness that consumed her
Away from the demons that haunted her
In the light

His rough hands on her skin sent chills down her spine
As he ripped her clothes off her body
She knew as she dared to look into his eyes,
Another beating was in line tonight

The tremors of fears had her jolted awake from the
nightmare she had before she could see the morning light

Silent sobs left her mouth as her eyes fell on the
blood-soaked sheets,
Biting her tongue, she moved to tend to her open wounds,
she felt his eyes on her which wanted her to crawl back
under the covers and hide

Her body stilled and she trembled in fear
A whimper escaped her lips as soon as she felt his fingers
on her face, wiping away the tears he cupped her cheek
as his thumb played with her trembling lip which was
bleeding from the bite

Wrapping his arms around her he picked her up from the bed
Ever so gently he put her Down in the tub
Soaking her body in the warm water he sat next to her
and bathe her
trying to wash away her fears with all his might

His rough fingers wrapped around her wrist
As he held the broken bottle
Of whisky he had been drinking all evening

Feeling powerful towering her petite frame
She stood her ground, trembling in fear
A rebellious cry of pain
came out of her mouth
When she saw him making a bloody trail
On her arm with that sharp end of the glass

Whimpering as he grabs a fistful of her hair
And force her to look at him
Drunken eyes that bore into hers
Filled with anger and hatred
Or was it pain that she saw?

Soon replaced by a smirk
Which once used to give her butterflies
And now makes her stomach churn in fear

Forcing a kiss on her lips, they were
Still as soft when they had first kissed
he remembers, as his hold softens
But gets clouded again by the resentment

Giving a love bite which he once loved
Seeing on her skin,
Turned a shade darker
Reminding her of her wrongs
Throwing the bottle towards the wall
He made his way towards the door

That now separated them
Into two different beings
That still belonged together
Carrying hatred and vengeance
One cold heart and another
A lost soul

Heart speaks to heart
Trying to make through the commotion in the dark

A bliss, tasted of forbidden fruit
He suffered the fate of Adam that made him prude

A train wreck he had every reason to fret
A Submissive shielded by the Dom
He had nothing to regret

Living in the cave of his Isolation
He sought to get out of this reverie

Silent screams they wanted to be heard
Walking on the thorns the feet bled...
The trail of blood was unseen & in silence they suffered

It was a battle cry
Satonic souls smiling wry
Demons won, and the hearts cried

Battered wills, couldn't fathom why
Traitor were the emotions that still tried

Incognito was the will power
Which showed up when the distress hovered

Hushed were the whispers
Which were never heard and in the thin air they dispersed

Lips were sealed and arms were tied
Rope of silence couldn't be loosened even if the
words tried

Scars showed even when they tried to hide
Specter of the haunted shadows

I hear screams
louder than thunder
i hear rain pouring
or is it your pain soaring?

I hear howls
in anger and agony, chilling growls
furious footsteps
nulling all the sounds

I see the storm
coming forth
but i feel no fear
for there's only ruins left
scattered in pieces, broken, shredded and torn

She lured him towards his misery
Arousing baits of lust
Wrapped in lace
And those sultry looks

Breathless nights of intense passion
She shivered as his fingers grazed on her skin
When he untied the laces
of her Corset and watching it drop
On the wooden floor with fashion

The stalking holder on her waist
Had him wanting to bite the soft skin
And leave his mark on her,
Claiming her as his

But the erotic romance ended before
It could start, the callous heart
Of the vixen he thought was a star
Fallen to his fate he couldn't blame but
Himself, for he had known

She was never his
The sweet charade was a mask
She wore, to get back to him
For what he had thought was forgotten in the past

Ishrat Parveen

He's stubborn as he gets
Tall talks and the promises
He never met

Delusional to have a fantasy
Of a lifetime to spend together
When he's still in the dark
Not wanting to let go of the
Secluded fictional charm

Just like their hopes
Their love didn't last long
Fierce desires, they fell again
For each other disarmed

She'd say the color of his eyes
were as deep as his soul
But she had never seen his eyes
Only the charcoal dark of his twisted
Soul

He told me a story
About the wolf and a girl
A beast on a rampage
Searching for his lost love

A love he could never claim
Before she could be his
She slipped away like sands of time,
The Time he couldn't tame

The loss fueled to his rage
When he destructed everything
Beautiful and brave
When the night came

He'd lie in his cave
And look at the moon
Finding answers to his questions
And fall into sleep
Dreaming of those glassy eyes

That looked at him
For the last time
Her blood soaked in his claws
As he Howled, holding
The lifeless body of his bride

The night didn't bring comfort anymore
Howls of sorrow, a great loss
Echoes in the forest
The pack has lost a wolf,
A healer in a frenzy
Scurrying away in the daunting night
Running away from the future
Leaving a newly found home
A home in the narrowed rivers
And she didn't know how to swim
Tripping on the roots of the old oak tree
The angry growl didn't make her slow down her speed

He believes in the folklore
To hide from the demons of his reality,
For he's cold, just like the ice
With walls hard like the diamond
And dark like a granite

Not knowing that the ice will melt
In the heat of his fire, for he's pyro
Burning and blinded by his own light

Succumbing to his own misery
Keeping the hard exterior
Burying the ashes of his expectations

She trespassed the sacred territory
Ruled by the ruthless Wolf
Cursed by the old witch,
Who once was his mate
Rejected by the one who
was supposed to protect her honor
Gave her the fate of banishment
From the grounds where they found each other
Knowing what's to come
A Lycan stands before her
Growling, demanding the reasons
Of committing a felony
As she stands before him
With a sadistic smile, seeing the
Tortured and a riled-up ex mate
But both fighting the inner battle
Of claiming who once was rejected
And cursed, paying for each other's mistakes

Loneliness brought them together
Yet they couldn't fight the feeling of being alone

Holding back so much in fear of loss
Taking a risk was too much to give a toss

Ignorance isn't bliss all the time
When giving into your feelings feels like a crime

Comfort turned into misery
Who's to blame for this treachery?

Rabid emotions going haywire
Brought them to set themselves on fire

Hold on, the voice whispered
And once again the heartbeats went erratic as the fond
memories triggered

She wasn't innocent
He was no saint
Unable to comprehend
All the effort went in vain

They were colors Ash & Steel
There was no brightness
With time they healed

Destructive Like a storm
They destroyed their own peace
There were no survivors
And then , the time took its leap

A decade later
The colors were still Ash and Steel
Coldhearted, they had everyone
Under their heels

That pasted smile
Which graced their lips when they saw each other
this time
They saw the shore in the storm together
Held in each other's arms tight
Is where they Found what was missing all this while

Once bitten, twice shy
They still yearned for each other with feelings none of
them could deny

Good and quickly seldom meet
the impatient hearts were striving to reach out to cool
each other's heat

They knew not to kindle with fire they couldn't put out
But the fire had already started
Steadily burning what they couldn't live without

The wonder lasted but nine days
And once again the fierce hearts were strays

The damaged heart couldn't love another damaged one
In this battle of broken hearts, one had to be the
stranded one

Your love...
Made me grin like a Cheshire cat
Selflessly selfish but I guess I was too weak to carry the
baggage that you had...?

Your love...
painful more than the happiness it harbors
Tortured by the silence of your lips that just murmurs

Your pain...
Screams in silence with echo that never ends
Ashamed was I to even dare to do something that could
help the broken heart mend

Your pain...
Which I was blind to notice in the fool's paradise
Perhaps perplexed with your distance that I didn't know if
I should fight or flight

Your distance...
When you stopped me from taking a step ahead
So I started talking to you in my diary instead

Red faced...
I was when I had put my heart into words...
made your silence even more of a torment than the
damage I did to you with my words

They lived in pretense
Carrying an aura, always tense
Lost in the steely thoughts of ever finding the one
true love

A love which was only theirs
To keep them safe and hidden from the
Prying eyes which always stares

Tangled in her curls, and
Caged in his arms
Making passionate love
Till no one remembers
What was the fight for

Leaving the room
In utter madness, screaming
But snuggling together
When the sun goes down

Being Iris to his pain
Just selfless love and
Nothing to gain but his heart
Marking as hers
As he imprinted his on hers
Till they see each other
Next time, on the judgment day

traces of her soul
she searched in his shadows
burned like an eternal flame
she didn't find her haven
in the beautiful meadows

in his love she bloomed
like a Sakura
endeavoring the beauty
of his affection, which soon faded

and she got lost
in the maze of his darkness
the love she once thought
was pure and kind

she became his Mistress
now seeking peace in her pain
and false hopes
while her faith withers
yet, she doesn't want to escape

As his unsaid comfort grew on her
She couldn't fathom why
A rogue would want to help her
Until she saw the scars
Inflicted by the time
And she knew it won't long
Before their walls shattered
With the silent screams
And a poised storm
Which soon will destroy
The kingdom of hearts
Causing a massacre
If growls and fire
For one is bounded by fate
And one is shackled by fears

She perked up when he smiled at her
Taking all her pain away in that moment
Giving her a forever that she longed for

He left as soon as he came by
Contemplating his decisions
If letting her get close was safe
Or yet another mistake,
Sardonic.. he smiled wry

But they coveted each other
An urge they couldn't control
To touch and make love
To each other's soul

Letting him go wasn't easy
To make a new start
But she had to be selfish
And think about her stupid heart

Perhaps she was a rough diamond
Or it was her own comforting lies
That made him cower away
Because for him it never rained
But only always poured

His efforts were futile
For he was too miserable to walk that extra mile
He didn't need any saving
But in his head he was tired and his hopes were draining

Fighting a lost cause
Because truth was bitter
And the comfort in lies
Was so liberating

That he didn't care for the wrongs
All that mattered was
To keep up the facade
And make himself more strong

Plethora of distractions
But still he fail to calm the tides
In his restless mind

No tunnels and no lights
With his fire he burns
And lighten up the footsteps
Not noticing

That his fire gave birth
To another warrior
Half wolf and half human
A mystic creature of the night

Blessed with powers
To heal the wounds
But bounded with the chains
Of an unknown power
An entity he couldn't fathom
But knew
That this is what his heart desired

He Runs away from reality
Like He refuse to see the clarity

He pulls off his facade so well
It won't be long when somebody will see through him and
he won't have to walk no more on sea shells

Beating himself over and over again
Thinks he's strong and undefeated
If only he'd take a look
and he'll see, he's not so unremitted

His heart covets the forbidden fruit
Carrying lethal storms he's a vicious brute

No comrades he'll be lost in his maze
No one to rely on... contingent but still remain dazed

he's a liar
in his love, there is no fire
yet he burns
in his own flames,
hating the world, who he blames

he lives on sandwiches and pizza
but talks like he drinks Irish beer
and dates a girl called Lisa

he stands on the mountain
of his sky-scraping ego
i do hope he step on a Lego

over works and rarely rest
he thinks his failures will make him
secondary to the best

lust is his escape
yet he longs for love
that's true to him
and become his slave

he cries at night
alone in his bed, a place of his own
where he doesn't have to hide

he thinks he knows it all
but fiction is his solace
where he can never fall

traces of her soul
she searched in his shadows
burned like an eternal flame
she didn't find her haven
in the beautiful meadows

in his love she bloomed
like a Sakura
endeavoring the beauty
of his affection, which soon faded

and she got lost
in the maze of his darkness
the love she once thought
was pure and kind

she became his Mistress
now seeking peace in her pain
and false hopes
while her faith withers
yet, she doesn't want to escape

He came, in a search for tomorrow
That no one had seen
A vision so blinding
That he couldn't heed

He was a warrior
Holding the leash of the Fenrir
And running in the wild

Darkness was his home
A safe haven
Where all his demons reside

A chaos of emotions
He hides a storm inside
A frisky wolf he is
But when the sun go down
His aura defines

A sinner in melancholy
A desire which isn't holy
He holds everything in his Reigns
Like nothing goes in vain

A catastrophic mystery
Of his own doom
Little did he know
His walls will break
And the destruction will be severe
But it won't be too soon

An impersonator
He fed her all the beautiful lies
Lies that she thought
Were unsaid promises
False hope where her fears could reside

It took too long
To see how she was so wrong
To believe In the empty promises
And a fictitious love which was never strong

A bond which she thought was real
Was a spell gone wrong
The wolf she thought was her mate
Turned out to be her doom
Who brought her a misery
She could never fathom

Walking on the broken pieces
She still followed his trail
To take back that part of her
Which she had lost
But finding him was
Getting lost in a Maze

Surrounded by the vicious Hounds
Who were lurking in the dark
Serving their master
Who was devious of them all

Her moans of ecstasy
Drove him crazy like a wolf in heat
He wanted to make her his
And take everything she had to offer
For him to please

As she wanted him
In every way possible
Heavy breathing and his whispered name
From her soft lips
Made his control on his resolve
Almost impossible

But he wanted her to last
All night long
Till her senses couldn't take it any longer
His sinful pleasure
Made her knees go weak

Please, she whispered in her soft moans
As he took her till her the sun came up
And she curled up next to him
Finding haven In his storm

But he knew he had to leave
This wasn't supposed to last this long
He had already prolonged his stay
Enough for her to fall in the darkness
Of his selfish needs and
In return she was only betrayed

She wasn't a damsel in distress
She wasn't a ray of sunshine
With light and a new hope

She was a massacre of thoughts
Sinking in the misery of her own wrongdoings
She was far from the moon
Hiding in her cave
Contemplating her own understandings

She listened to no one
Livid and lost
Still not enough
She was confused from the start

Still dreamy and hopeful
She'd strive to go by in peace
Living in tomorrows
Never wanting the colossal
Day dreams to cease

Torpe, he'd stare at her from afar
Not aware that she was a fallen star
But he could see that she was in a battle against her
demons... a never-ending war

He wasn't a knight,
He wanted to be her warrior
And stand by her side until everything became alright

She'd see him every night
Watching her trying to figure out why she was so uptight but,
She saw him as a threat like everyone else around her and
would wonder
What would he want her for?

She felt exposed with his every stare
Afraid that maybe he was able to figure her out.
Threatened that it'd be easier for him to play with her mind
But this time she didn't care for this time she wasn't left
with anything to spare

She had no right, she had no say
He was like a strong wind
Wherever he blew that's where
she swayed

She saw her love in the dark nights
When the clouds covered the sky
Like sheets of sorrow
A dreadful silence in the night sky
Weighing down in the pain
Which wasn't there's but borrowed

When The pink hue in the sky beautifies
Every evening as the lost lovers unites
A blush rose into her cheeks
Awaiting the arrival of her lover

like the evening sky awaits her moon
But the howling of the Winds is heard
And the lost lovers separate yet again
When the new moon arises and hidden from the naked eyes
The rain pours,
The lovers cry, drifting into their own darkness, lonely
heart cries

She didn't need no saving
She wanted to feel safe
But she couldn't ignore the craving
Which she needed to satiate

In his Auras she wanted to thrive
When he strengthened her wills
With his battered self
But he wasn't a selfless man

He had tricks up his sleeves
Playing his cards right
He knew he'd never
Allow her to leave

A manipulative lover
They both were a perfect fit
Knowing what's on each other's mind
An essence too strong
To ignore the gist

She's quiet, humming the symphony
That her wailing heart desires
Forbidden is the love
So she stays afar, waiting

If ever the gates open
And she's allowed in
Not a wolf right now
But a melody of sorrows

She's a human after all
Living in her tomorrows
Awaiting the fantasy
Of a fictional romance

Adorned in white lace
Red lips that he wanted to kiss
Wild curls sprawled on the satin sheets
Looking like his wildest fantasy coming to life

Came to an end too quick
with broken promises
Of many enticing tomorrows
in one frenzied night

He's scared
And she's scared for him
Thinking of ways to bring him
Out of the grim

Fate is a foe
Smirking at the lost lovers
Denial is better
Forgetting is better than to suffer

But will she forget?
The love that she never got
The safe embrace of his arms
Seeking comfort
In his wilting heart

But she'll keep him
Until she see him again
In an hourglass pendant
Close to her heart

So he knows she's safe
Living a life in masquerade
Seeking normalcy and quiet
Feeding on the hate

He was a cursed wolf
Who was betrayed by the fate
Filled with melancholy
He carried too much hate

For himself and the world
But he made her his escape
A woman herself a misery
Couldn't ease out his pain

But he sought comfort
In her withered presence
A dime a dozen, her
Worth was measured
In the silence of his gentry

She submitted in his presence
For his aura had always been so tense
And when he would shift into his wolf
She'd see the loving mate
Whom she always misunderstood

Show me your scars
Not the one on your skin
But the ones on your soul

The ones that were inflicted by you
Not the ones by the world
The ones that made you mystery
That made you an epiphany
Of a broken record
Sending chills to the core

Show me your demons
Because they know mine
They protect you like a second skin
Is that why you're always defensive?
Like breaking the wall is a crime

A wall adorned by the thorns
Of nightmares of past and hate
Yet you never lose your charm
A beautiful pretense
Of deception you could create

We turned the page
We burned the book
But the memoirs of hearts
Couldn't be let off the hook

Writing love letters in the clouds
Watching them fade away
But when it rained
We tasted them on our lips
On a cold rainy day

Chasing the moon
And it ran faster
Just like your heart
When I thought I was close
I found myself, where
I had started the walk

Cold feet and slippery road
When the lights go out
You'd still remain The one
my heart would always choose

She waits, for only waiting has she known
he lies so she stays and kill his void
He is more than his words
A charming imposter, of the
most beautiful dream she ever had

An incarnation of his own fallen hopes
Built with a chilling nightmare
That she fears and love at the same time

A limping werewolf who leaves the trail
Of blood, which is not red anymore
But turned a shade of grey

his wolf have been gone too long
And now he is only a human
Walking slowly, where she has taken refuge

In the cave, Behind the waterfall
Where he saw her on her first shift
Their sacred place, their safe haven

Ishrat Parveen

Their bond was pledged in secrecy
One with a fearless heart,
Another was a trickster who played his charm

Falling for the mistake
He got played himself
By the untethered desires
And lust for hearts

To mend what was broken
He went in the dark
Into an abyss too far
Far away from her

But she was a believer
So she believed in the lies too
Holding on to the broken promises
To save the traitor heart

She followed him
Into the alleys where
The only light was the moon
Who was too hiding
Behind the blanket
Of the dark clouds

Tell me another lie
For the lies only I have known
Hopes of an eternity
In the charades of silence
Withholding the emotions
Of the love so tiring
Searching for the memories
Buried long ago
To fuel the fire
Which had turned into the ashes
Of bitter love, but still the sweetest
For it's the true love, that never loses hope

Denying the bond so effortlessly
Like you knew what you were doing
But how would you break the bond
When your heart skips a beat
every time your wolf calls for her

Your mate you wished for secretly
To the goddess of the makers
When you'd look at the moon at night
Praying the star falls right

But the constellation was
Disrupted, but you're a lionheart
Living in the irony of
Fate ruled by the fallen heart
And healing wounds
But you know you can't break
The bond, for its something
Which you cannot control or manipulate

It's real, the scars on your soul
The year stains on you shirt that you
Hide from people so they may not see
You at your vulnerable,
It's real, when you hold on to everything just so you won't
give up on yourself,
It did you give up already?
Because you got tired fighting
To keep what belonged to you
Or did it ever?
you wouldn't let another
Take it from you so quick as it came
Perhaps it was an affair of the night
Where you make the promises of the worlds
But fear the transparency in the eyes
Of the one who once was unsullied
Then corrupted by the nightmares of
The storms combined

A figment of her imagination
Lurking in the shadows
Of her nightmares,
Devil in a tuxedo
Feeding on the fears
With prowess like he depends on it
Giving him the pleasure
He got from no other soul
Demanding like he owns it
And she gives as though
She knows that's what
She's supposed to do
To Bring him pleasure from her sorrows

Two shadows in love profound
Couldn't get enough of what they had found

Writhing in pain all those years
Came to an end
When the fierce hearts found their anchors

Lost in each other's eyes for a lifetime
Finding the solace in each other's arm,
Where everything felt so right

Reaching for the kiss
Which was long awaited
Stolen by the moment when the eyes opened from the
dream that she'd always hated

Tearing out the night he came
Escaping from the walls his demons had built so high

Searching for his love everywhere
In the darkest forests to the corner of the earth but
couldn't find her to no avail

Wallowing inside he howled to the moon
Crying to the goddess, accusing her for taking his love
away from him so soon

Forgiveness was in his repentance
When the loss of love brought the beast on his knees

His rejection was a blessing in disguise
That he now knew the value of his mate that filled his
missing pieces

Yearning for the love he turned his back on, he got his
everything back when he found his little mate sleeping on
the same bed where he had left her

Now lying next to her, holding her tight as the tears
left his eyes taking in the damage, he had done to
both of them

Everything dissipated when he felt the hesitant arm
wrapping around his torso and he brought her closer
inhaling her scent hiding his face in her dark tresses

Tears running along he fell asleep into the dark abyss
finding comfort in her closeness, and to him his love
never felt so deep

And now I lay in your arms
Away from all the harms

Maybe now my scars will fade away
Thinking I breath in your scent
Calming my restless senses

I wake up to see you looking at me
Your eyes burning into my soul
Lowering my gaze, I snuggle closer
In your embrace where I want to be

Playful nibbles and bites
In your love I thrive
You became my home
My wolf, where all my sweetest memories reside

Their love was like an eternal fire
Which only ever increased

They would fight like enraged wolves
In each other's arms they'd come back to sleep

They would love like they knew they were together
In the kingdom of souls

When they were lost between the devil
And the deep blue sea,

The hope of finding each other kept them going
To find each other they sailed close to wind

Every cloud has a silver lining
And she was his moon, hiding behind those clouds

Lightening his withered and torn soul
After the centuries of being kept apart

Ishrat Parveen

his Aura was epiphany,
he wore it like a duvet,
of calm and serenity

lust he chases
perhaps, he likes to get lost in the maze
there's no period
in his unchaste

his esquire is dainty
or is it his heart?
lone and chaste...

slow dancing in the masquerade
of souls,
a place where whom, no-one knows

quenching thirst of his desires
his rebellious heart forlorn
ignorance is bliss
yet he yearns to seize the moment before its gone

She pulled him closer
Like the distance wasn't enough
When he thrusted

Wrapping her legs around him
As she grinded her burning core
In ecstasy against him

If this was how it felt
She never wanted him to stop
Bringing her pleasure in
The ways she couldn't imagine

She got on her knees
And gave him what they both
Had been wanted for so long

He stroked her hair
When she matched the pace of her hand with her tongue
And when he couldn't take no more
He pulled her up again
And this time
He took her against the wall

He looked into those dark orbs
Where he saw the reflection of
The moon he always wanted to reach

And in that moment, he realized
It's wasn't the moon he wanted
What he wanted was standing in front
In this very moment

But far away from his reach
Farther than his arms could reach
So, he savored the moment
Before it slipped away
Once again, before he could tell her to stay

He knew she was long gone
The epiphany was so surreal
That he forgot about the world
And marked what was his
As his imprinted his mark
On her neck

Knowing that she was his
Even though she bore someone else's child
He'd still claim his mate
The one for whom he waited
An eternity fighting his demons
And this she'll be his
For the lifetime

Fisting her hair, he pulled her close
Emotions gone crazy
Feelings were haywire
He wanted to devour her
Like she was a drug he had always desired

Wrapping her legs around him
She grinded against his flesh
Skin on skin but the lust
Didn't seem to go any less

Covered in sheets he pulled her close
Resting his head on her Bossom
They still craved for more
Endless hours of sensual love making
In the wildest ways

They were still hot for each other
Wanting more and more
In every way possible
Like the lust was still underdose

A smile played on her lips
He gazed and desired to kiss that little beauty spot above
her lip that he'd always failed to notice

And how she'd always frown
Lost in her deranged thoughts
Which always ended in a tsunami
But he never tried to save her and let her drown

His heart swelled with pride
As he took a look again at his wife
The woman who brought him out of his darkness where
he always wanted to reside

But now his world fell apart, as he saw
Her succumbing to the darkness
He secured her in the safe embrace of his arms wrapping
them around her like a harness

He's like the color purple
His grandeur aura wraps him
In a safe circle

Where he's protected
From the illusions
Of the things unknown
And the things unsaid

He's powerful holding his ground
A mysterious phoenix
Who nobody saw
He was feral and unbound

Living in his manor
Surrounded by souls
Still finding a safe haven
To burn into ashes again

In the haven
Where the truth unfolds
With the self-deceived lies
And a pride to withhold

He sits in the box seat,
Holding his cards right
Ready to Ace his game
That never leaving smirk on his
Chiseled face,
Following her every move
As she slowly walks towards her doom
Sighing in relief when his claws
Dug into her skin
Deep enough to leave a mark
As his fangs caressed the nape of her neck
Ready to claim what is his
Pulling her hair, she cranes her neck
Giving him a better access,
That moan of approval didn't go unnoticed
And he smiles faintly, content at her approval
Not waiting a second more to delay
And begin a story that has always been a cliché

The soft whisper in his lazy morning voice
Almost made her knees go weak
He snuck his hand quick
Between her thighs, as she squeezed
Them keeping his hand in place

Nibbling on her ear he was enjoying
His morning teasing and
Working her up till she's putty in his hands
Screaming his name when
Her back arches and he'd give her
The pleasure for being a good girl

Her moans demanded more
When he slowly played with her
Hidden jewel, fingers deep inside
Preparing her for the fuck
But she is anything but patient
With his slow and torturous tease

she spread her legs
Turning over and planting
A fierce kiss on his smirking lips
Biting and sucking as his fingers
Worked, taking her high
But not giving her what she wants

As her body convulses
And right then he straddles her
Forcing his thick hot flesh
A moan of approval when he feels her warmth
Around his throbbing hard on

His tongue dominates her mouth
Like his thrusts of possession
Claiming what's his for
the hours of ecstasy and wilderness
She submits to him, from him
There's no getaway

Tell me a story in black and white
Satin sheets and a feather
Teasing skin in the dark night

Tight enough to leave the marks
In the morning, loose enough
To make me squirm and beg for more
Pleasure so enticing

No screams but muffled cries
Loud moans in rhythm
With the groans of the lover
When our bodies grind

Sheer lust scented with love
Inked with the pain,
Handled with care
In the deceitful night of love
Did not go in vain

Her face glowed in the light of those
Bright fairy lights,
Feeling like a firefly she was giddy
With the unperturbed feeling of
Being lost again in the night

A night where all the stars were aligned
As if they gathered to see her
Joy in her overwhelmed self
Where no more fear she had to hide

A withering flame who was
Dancing in the cold winds
Melting the snow and engulfing
The vapors as they rose above
Casting another beautiful glow

Her arrival brings the serenity
and the calm that he seeks
A fragile luxe beauty Lasting
for a few days Much to his dismay,
Beautifying his world in the subtle
colors of her feminine passion
That he wants to keep all to himself
till her last petal falls - Sakura

His obsidian orbs captured the beauty of his thoughts
A love that's out of the ark which sailed under the
false colors,
Incognito in the eyes of his Querida

His intelligence is as enticing as his mysterious persona
Hiding secrets of the unknown in the full moon he runs wild
Colossal form of his coal black wolf reverberates the
howl in the
Starry night, announcing his arrival to his destiny
Who waits,
Arrayed in the silver cloak of serenity

A sorceress, wondering in the wild
Succoring the wounded
In the war of the underworld
But now the time to summon
The one who'd put an end to this
Arose, from the flames he was born
To be the Saviour of the wild
Little did he know, he would

Also find the one who was Destined
For him, the one who summoned him...
Hiding under the cloak of darkness
Running away for eons, away from him
Into the abyss where her fears reside

Tell me a lie, a lie that I've been yearning to hear,
For the truth hold no promises anymore.

He wonders in the search of
An Auburn beauty...A patron of love
In the dry autumn evenings
When she glows in the sunset
Casting a Striking hue of her shadow
On his withered face,
Giving him the strength,
Peace in his chaos When his world shakes.
- Maple leaf

Feeble and miserable Our souls are tired and torn,
Let me be the cure of your sorrows Let me be your home.

He followed her into the dark abyss
Of her unsound mind,
Not knowing which way to follow
But the scent of her Tresses
Was his wayward guide.

Every lipshade on her plump petals tells a story,
Of a fierce flower...of a fierce heart.

He looks at the jar with a warm smile every night
Before falling asleep, she may have gone but her
heart that he kept in that jar when he murdered
her always reminded him of her presence.

Let her mourn in her darkness,
for when she illuminates,
she'll shine like a pole star
and never lose that light again.

Her Fiend Curls were a reflection of her disheveled emotions.

He painted her with colors her skin had never seen...
Red, blue and purple. Crippling her soul and
incapacitating her pride.

Some of us strive to find the reality in the love that
is fiction

He was that dark cloud who came to quench
the draught in her heart. And left after pouring
some rain. For he moved with the winds and she
was the ground that always remained rooted
nurturing with a selfless heart.

She hides her chaos under the cloak of serenity.

Dreaming of a stranger in the nights forlorn,
His ambiguity so captivating A beautiful maze
Which never promised her a dawn.

Stars don't shine anymore
Moon doesn't come out anymore
You loved the darkness so much
Now you're searching for your reflection,
Lost in the darkness of your own echo.

There are nights when I wear my anxiety like a blanket

I don't look for the light at the end of the tunnel. I am
the light

To fall asleep in your arms,
listening to your thumping heart...
In the dusk of an autumn evening as our heartbeats
sync in the rhythm of a sacred song

He creates a song with the hymn of his chaos, which she
sings to him in a melody sublime

Come to me like an old hidden wound,
Stay with me Like a wolf cry to the full moon.
Bittersweet pain Like I slip in the rains.
Too close but too far Like the train at my lost station
which never came.

I am in love with the moon for it walks
with me holding my hand in the dark alleys
of bleeding red nights. For the sun is too
blinded by its own lights to ever leave it's
path and take a step for me

He whispered the unsaid, his
warm breath fanning her cheek
blowing a few rebel strands of
her dark curls, this moment he shall keep.
feeling safe he vented to her,
Knowing she's asleep.
he couldn't turn his back now
But his fears ran skin deep

In the awake of twilight, they come forth,
Riding the ravenous hounds
Amassing the wondering souls
Who lost their way
In the frazzled masses of
The heedless souls

Under the midnight blue sky full of fireworks,
I bring the zircons of frozen tears into the
Auburn dawns of fiery tomorrows

And every fleeting moment with you took a part of me,
leaving me a little emptier that I could hear the echoes of
my mourning heart...

Let me put my arms around you
Let's share some warmth
My warm skin and your cold heart
Let me calm your storm
Let me be your sun
For I won't burn you
My love, I burn in you

A love affair of the fall.
They wrote their love stories in the longest night before
they ended all.

Long walks after midnight brings me peace...
Or maybe it's the chaos in my mind seeking quite in the
moonlit sidewalks.

Looking for myself in the burnt pages of my past, waiting for a phoenix to be born...

I want to stay in the past. It's comforting there, it's like a rough blanket but keeps me warm nonetheless.

We build a bridge and set it on fire
With flames that engulfs all our desires
Leaving us with the ashes of the burnt
Backbones, striving to be deserved
In the eyes of broken Whilst carrying our own
Broken pieces. Walking into the chasm of dreams
Leaving the trail of pieces behind Hoping someone
would follow,
Someone did follow Walking on the shards of
broken pieces
To chastise the foolish soul and pleasure their own
cynical interest

I go for walks every day, on same path where you used to walk. Following the trail of your footsteps to fill the void...

It's a maze of mediocrity Where she chases the untouched, wearing a lop-sided grin.

He's an imposter with the sultry Charm, he's composed
But depicts a hoax of Hot-blooded deceits of
Velvety harms.
Never disarmed by the inane Logics of his tethered
selfish heart,
So, he lies to himself as though he pulls the strings of the
rebellious heart.

She writes her flaws
With an ink of epiphanies
Matted with the dirt
Of sorrows and treachery

Nursing wounds
Inflicted by the bittersweet desires
Lost in his obsidian orbs
Set ablaze like an eternal pyre

It's a poison she drinks
That burns her soul
Writhing in misery
Which makes her feel whole

She wasn't his dream that he dreamt of
In the lonesome nights
She was his inspiration
When he was lost
His light when it was pitch dark
For he couldn't stay in the dark forever
Letting go of the hatred
That he had built up in purgatory
Of his heart, worn out
And fallen apart

He holds the reigns of his own destiny
Yet he finds someone to blame
He is his own nemesis
In his denials he feels safe

He looks for chaos
In the serenity of his heart
Where the mind is reaping havoc
His heart yearns of the peace

His scars seemed perfect
When she kissed them
Under the dimmed lights
Tracing them with her fingers
He shivered under her gentle touch
The utter vulnerability in his eyes
And her come hither look
Never wanted her to go out of his sight

Tell me the truth
One you had been running away from
Or the one you are in denial of
Or the one which scares you the most
A blasphemy, which shows a different host
A beautifully told lie, making them think
They should never try
To bring those walls down
For when they break
He knew,
They all will drown

He loved to count the freckles
On her face, ones he adored
Before, when they were
Not covered in bruises
Bruises that he gave her
A stigma of his vile
Brutal soul, an embrace
That once she loved
Now gave her an uncanny feel

He was her mate
From the most coveted dream
As surreal as a prophecy
As promising as an enchanting spell
But he became her curse
A doom to which she got lured
She was brave but paralyzed
Where to run or to whom
She couldn't decide
Nothing last forever
Her wolf recites
She found what she needed
In herself, her chastity her wolf

He's the one, so she says
Listening to her wolf
Who's drunk in his love
She knows if or not he stays

For he is a wild spirit
Who leaps in the air leaving her stunned
In darkness he lurks
Waiting for the one
He had always wanted to return

The horizon looks mesmerizing
Amber, just like the fire within you
So beautifully spreading across the sky
Just like the darkness within you
Enveloping you like a blanket

She waits for tomorrow
Where all the demons reside
Ones whom she wants to run to
To have those claws wrapped around her
Not to harm her but to protect
For the beast awaits
For the one who was lost
And abandoned far away

It's not the idea
But an unrealistic dream
An unsaid wish
Caressed by the silence
Of the unnerved egos

Dancing shadows in the fire
Burning the village
Protected by the songs of the hearts
Engulfed in the smoke of desires
Losing its way in the dark

A beautiful moment created under the stars
Ruined by the ghosts of the past
Running away from her future again
When he looked away
Into the storm, which never seemed to pass

There is always a hidden motive
In the eyes of the beholder
He who only knows to demand
Obedience of his maiden

There is an unsaid promise
she abides by till she remembers
Falling for the charades
Of the incapable geezer

There is chaos in solitude
Sipping on the poison of the rotten souls
Feeding off the battered wills
A dementor of the fallen hopes

and that is when I made love with the
Darkness,
Letting go of the fears and wearing them as a
Cloak of serenity
Which I once wore like shackles.

Here I felt safe and protected
the cold kept me warm like
I am resting in a cocoon
Spun by the nightmares
Which ones had me praying
To sought protection.

I used to love shades of black and grey,
And now my eyes wanders searching for brighter colors.
Perhaps I have evolved into a colorful mess.

It's always the witty men,
Oh, so charming and so cheesy.
Not that I don't like cheese,
but not when it gets too sleazy.

To the road with a dead end,
I wandered off, looking for myself
In the day with my flashlight on.
Darker it got as I got closer,
Or maybe it was me losing my sight
As my shadow left me,
on the route and I had nowhere to hide.

You're my midnight poem
I always love to read
My bedtime prayer
My favorite plushy
Next to me, which i always love to keep.

Th barbed wires
That surrounds your walls
Have the dried up blood
Of the ones who tried to climb them
Whilst you watch them
Sitting in the dark
Devouring that glass of whisky
Watching them giving up
On the hopes and promises
Tied with the loose knot
then falling to the grounds
Complaining, how difficult the climb was.

His hard gaze fell upon
The long locks, that swayed
In the air, as if they're dancing.
His fingers itched to run
Through them
As he held her and
Kissed her in the balcony
Of her room which was lit
By the moonlight
Their heartbeats were synched
Beating like a drum
Hands rummaging to get rid
of every piece of fabric that was in between, her
soft moans
That demanded more of him
Were like a sweet serenade
That his love bites appreciated.
Into the wild rendezvous
He ravished his beloved
Hushed cloying whispers
She wasn't perturbed,
For it felt safe, with him
She was no more unnerved.

He loathes the fate
Like they are sworn enemies,
But she still loved him like an old lover who
Had committed a felony
But their love was cursed, for he never wanted
To be hers, she had waited too long
In his wait she was forlorn

Hearing her thoughts
he comes apart at the seams
For there's no melodies
Only deafening screams.
He still tries to cork up something
To provide a momentarily comfort
But it all goes in vain,
For she sees through it all
And allow the silence to consume
The destructive rabid thoughts.

Her eyes held the joys of spring
Reading the letter of her beloved
That she waited to arrive for so long
For there was always something about
The love letters, keeping her antsy
To read the unsaid thoughts
Of his vulnerable thoughts

He held her so tight
Like his life was depended on it
Burning her in his fire
Yet there were no burns
But only the warmth
In the embrace of
The beloved forlorn
Endeavoring the comfort
To the lost soul who sought
Comfort in the arms of his
Partner, his kryptonite and his strength
She gave him strength
Even when his fire burned out
That fire long gone
And he lost his pace
But she brought back his fire
More lethal and ravenous
When she gave him her fire
With a selfless heart
which had no desire

9 798888 156261